To ....

With love from

....

W9-CQF-354

BBC CHILDREN'S BOOKS
Published by the Penguin Group
Penguin Books Ltd, 80 Strand, London, WC2R ORL, England
Published by BBC Children's Books, 2005
Text and design © Children's Character Books, 2005
1 3 5 7 9 10 8 6 4 2
BBC & logo © and ™ BBC 1996
Pingu © The Pygos Group 2005
With thanks to HOT Animation
www.pingu.com

Printed in China
ISBN 1 405 90065 2 & 9 781405 900652

Pingu's Best Friend

Pingu is a very
friendly penguin...

he has lots of friends.

His girlfriend, Pingi,
is very nice.

Pingu thinks she's lovely!

Pingo is good to play with too...

but he can be a bit
accident-prone!

Even little sister Pinga can be fun sometimes!

His very best friend
of all though, is
Robby the seal!

Being best friends is great!

Pingu and Robby
love camping out...

midnight feasts...

and having snowball fights!

They get up to lots of mischief together...

and sometimes they get into trouble...

but they are
always very sorry for
being naughty!

Whenever Pingu has a great idea...

Robby is always there to lend a flipper.

Sometimes though,
even the best plans...

end in disaster!

Despite being best friends...

they can be very competitive!

Even Robby and
Pingu argue from
time to time...

but they always make up in the end!

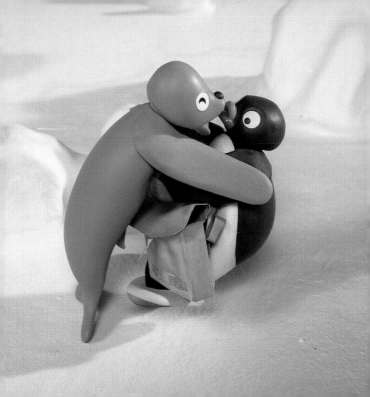

Best friends forever!